FIRST AID

Brian R. Ward

Series consultant:
Dr Alan Maryon-Davis
MB, BChir, MSc, MRCP, FFCM

LIFE GUIDES

Franklin Watts
London · New York · Toronto · Sydney

First published in 1987 by
Franklin Watts
12a Golden Square
London W1

First published in the USA by
Franklin Watts Inc.
387 Park Avenue South
New York, N.Y. 10016

First published in Australia by
Franklin Watts Australia
14 Mars Road
Lane Cove
New South Wales 2066

UK ISBN: 0 86313 453 X
US ISBN: 0-531-10260-2
Library of Congress Catalog Card No: 86-50356

Design: Howard Dyke

Picture research: Anne-Marie Ehrlich

Illustrations:
Andrew Aloof, Dick Bonson, Howard Dyke, Sally
Launder, Nick May.

Photographs:
Sally and Richard Greenhill 40
Sporting Pictures 39

Printed in Belgium

Contents

Introduction

A book of this sort cannot describe the specialized forms of first aid needed to cope with every injury. If you want to know more, proper first-aid training is available from several first-aid organizations.

What is first aid? And why should you need to know how to give first aid? First aid is exactly what it seems. It is the help *first* given to an ill or injured person, before regular medical aid can be obtained.

First aid has several very simple but important objectives. First, and obviously most important, is to save life. Next is the need to prevent the illness or injury from getting worse. The final objective is to speed the recovery of the victim.

Accidents can be caused by a huge number of circumstances, and can happen at home, at school, on the road, or anywhere else.

Some accidents threaten life, and this book outlines some simple methods of first aid which could help you save the life of a victim. It also describes many first-aid procedures for very common but minor injuries like cuts, bruises and splinters. Quite often, if first aid is carried out properly for these injuries, no further medical treatment will be necessary.

First aid is the help given to a person who has suffered an injury. It is given before regular medical treatment can be obtained. If carried out properly, first aid can prevent the injury from getting worse, and can speed recovery.

What to do in an emergency

When you are faced with an accident, or with someone who has been taken ill, don't just rush in to start first aid. Take a moment to assess the situation properly. You must look around to be sure that you are not going to endanger yourself or the victim. If there has been a road accident, for example, you will need to get someone else to stop or control the traffic before you begin first aid. In other types of accident, you may need to make sure that the victim is not threatened by fire or by gas. And if a person has received an electric shock, you must be very sure that you do not risk electrocution yourself.

Perhaps several people have been hurt. Whom will you help first? Obviously you must begin first aid with the person most seriously hurt, and this means examining the victims to see if their injuries threaten life.

When there has been an accident, it is important to organize first aid properly. Without being officious, you must ask for help and decide how the injury should be treated. If several people are involved, you must decide who needs treatment most urgently. And most important, you must call the emergency services for medical help.

Practical help at an accident

Sending for help
When you send people to call for assistance, make sure they carry out all of these steps:
1 Telephone the emergency services. This can be done using a special number or through the operator.
2 Give the telephone number in case they get cut off.
3 Give the fullest possible description of the accident, the state of the victim, and how to reach the site of the incident.
4 Don't hang up until after the person answering the emergency call has done so, in case there are more questions to be answered.
5 Report back to you that the emergency call has been made.

Unless a victim is only slightly hurt, you must establish some treatment priorities. These are very important and could save a life, especially if the victim is unconscious.

There is a simple code to help you remember the three first-aid principles:

A is for **airway**.

B is for breathing.

C is for circulation of the blood.

Check that the victim's airway is clear so that air can reach the lungs (see pages 10–11).

Check that the victim is breathing. If not, breathing must be restored immediately with **mouth-to-mouth resuscitation** (see pages 14–15).

Make sure that the victim's heart is beating. If the heart has stopped, you must immediately begin **external heart compression** (see pages 16–17). If the victim is bleeding, you must try to control the loss of blood (see pages 22–3). You may also have to treat the victim for **shock** (see pages 24–5).

If other people are around, get them to help. Most important of all is to send for medical help.

Calling for medical help in an emergency must be done properly. Give a clear message, and make absolutely sure that the emergency services know what to expect when they arrive at the accident so that they can bring the proper equipment.

9

Clearing the airway

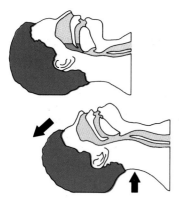

In an unconscious victim, the tongue may drop back into the throat, obstructing breathing.

When the head is tilted back, the tongue is lifted clear, opening the airway.

If the victim is unconscious, you must first make sure that nothing is blocking the victim's airway.

The airway is the passage that leads from the mouth, nose and throat to the windpipe. If it is blocked, air cannot reach the lungs. The victim's tongue may have fallen back and blocked the airway, or there may be other obstructions such as vomit. A person who is deeply unconscious cannot cough to clear blockages and will die within minutes unless the obstruction is cleared.

To open the airway, tilt the victim's head right back with one hand on the forehead and one under the neck. Then push the chin up. This lifts the tongue clear of the back of the throat and usually allows breathing to start again.

Check breathing by placing your cheek alongside the victim's mouth, feeling and listening for breath and looking along the chest to see whether it is rising and falling.

If the victim is still not breathing, turn the head to one side, open the mouth and sweep your fingers around inside to hook out any food, dentures or vomit which might be blocking the airway.

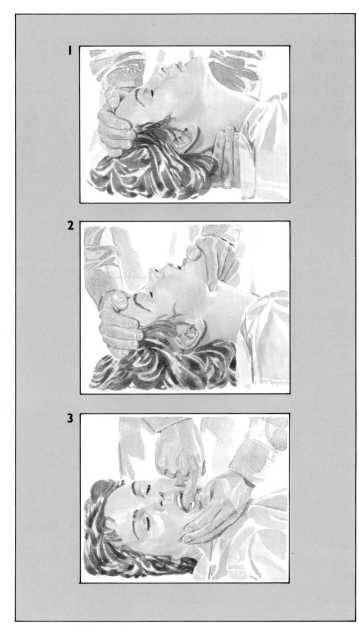

1 Place one hand on the forehead and the other under the neck of the victim, tilting the head right back.
2 Push the chin upwards, so that the tongue is lifted away from the back of the throat.
3 If the victim is still not breathing, turn the head to one side, and sweep a finger around inside the mouth to remove any obstructions.

  If the victim starts to breathe at any stage, turn into the recovery position.

The recovery position

Once the victim is breathing properly again, they must be placed in a position where they can remain safely until help arrives.

Putting a victim into the **recovery position** makes sure that the airway is kept open and that the tongue cannot drop back to block the throat. Any vomit can drain out of the mouth without causing a blockage. The recovery position also prevents the victim from rolling over and causing further injury.

Victims must be placed in the recovery position if they are unconscious or semi-conscious, but they must still be watched carefully to make sure that their breathing does not deteriorate and that the heart continues to beat properly.

An unconscious victim who is breathing properly, and whose heart is beating, must be placed in the recovery position as shown here. This ensures that they will continue to breathe properly, without the tongue blocking their throat, or being choked by vomit.

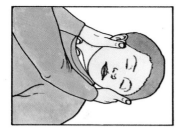

1 Kneel at the side of the victim, turn the head to one side, and tilt it back.

2 Lay the nearest arm along the victim's side, and tuck his hand under his buttock.

3 Lay the other arm over the victim's chest. Lift the far leg, and cross it over the nearest leg.

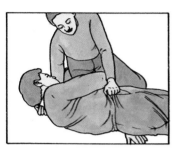

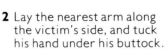

4 Support the victim's head with one hand. Grip the clothes over the furthest hip, pulling the victim toward you so that he rolls on to his side.

5 Make sure the head is comfortably on its side, and well tilted back to keep the airway open.

6 Raise the uppermost arm and leg to stop the victim rolling right over. Straighten the lower arm behind the victim to stop him rolling on his back.

If the victim has broken limbs, or if you suspect back or neck injury, you should not roll them into the recovery position as this could mean further damage. Instead you should hold their head back and their chin up to keep the airway open.

The proper technique for turning a victim into the recovery position is shown above. It needs to be learned and practiced, as an unconscious adult can be very difficult to move.

Once the victim is in the recovery position, you can treat any minor injuries.

Restoring breathing

If, after clearing the airway, breathing does not start immediately, you must waste no time in beginning mouth-to-mouth resuscitation.

This involves gently blowing air from your own lungs into the lungs of the victim. There is enough oxygen left in the air you breathe out to keep the victim alive. The technique can be safely carried out on almost all victims, even the youngest babies.

In an adult, the nose is pinched shut, and air is blown steadily into the mouth. But in babies, it is easier to cover the child's nose and mouth with your own mouth, and you must blow only gently to avoid damaging their lungs. Because of the position of your head while giving artificial resuscitation, you can easily watch the victim's chest to see that it is rising as you blow. This confirms that the airway is open, and that air is entering the lungs.

Never waste time looking for hidden obstructions before beginning artificial resuscitation, but get four good breaths into the victim's lungs as soon as possible.

1 To carry out mouth-to-mouth resuscitation, pinch the victim's nostrils shut. Take a deep breath, and seal your lips round the mouth of the victim. Make sure that the victim's head is tilted back, keeping the airway open.

2 Blow steadily into the victim's mouth. Lift your mouth away and watch to see if the chest is now falling as air is breathed out. Repeat the process three more times, then check that the heart is beating. If so, continue.

3 Give a breath every 5 seconds to an adult and every 3 or 4 seconds to a child. When the victim begins to breathe unaided, turn to the recovery position. If the heart has stopped, you must immediately begin external heart compression (see page 16).

When the heart has stopped

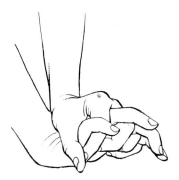

The clasped hands are used to apply pressure to the breastbone. Place one hand on top of the other, and lace the fingers firmly together.

If you have cleared the victim's airway and tried mouth-to-mouth resuscitation, and the victim is still not breathing, you must quickly check that the heart is beating.

Find the victim's Adam's apple in the throat, and slide your finger tips gently to one side of it, into the hollow between the Adam's apple and the large neck muscles. Do not press hard! You should be able to feel the **pulse**. If there is no pulse, the victim's face and lips will be bluish in color. If you are sure that the heart is not beating, you must use the technique of external heart compression to restart it. This should be combined with mouth-to-mouth resuscitation until the heart has started again.

Heart compressions are given by pressing rhythmically on the breastbone or **sternum**, in the middle of the chest. It is important to press on the proper part of the breastbone, so that pressure is applied to the heart. The breastbone runs from the notch between the ribs just below the throat down to the gap between the ribs, over the abdomen.

Find the breastbone, and roughly measure its center point. You will have to apply pressure to the middle of the lower half. Follow the instructions given on the right.

Follow the instructions given on the right.

Important
Never use external heart compression on a person whose heart is beating, as this can cause serious damage.

Lay the victim flat on his back and kneel alongside. Locate the center of the breastbone, and place your interlaced hands on the center of the lower half. Keeping your arms straight, lean forward so that you press the breastbone down about 5 cm (2 in). Release the pressure, then repeat, continuing about 80 times each minute. You can count "One and two, one and two" under your breath to time yourself. Pause after each 15 presses to give two breaths of mouth-to-mouth resuscitation. Then continue with the chest compression until the pulse restarts. If this occurs, **stop compression immediately** and continue with mouth-to-mouth. Then turn the victim to the recovery position.

Drowning and asphyxiation

There are many accidents which can cause breathing to stop. And these accidents can be dangerous for the first aider. You will first have to remove the victim from the dangerous situation, or take steps to reduce the danger.

Suffocation

This occurs when air is prevented from reaching the air passages. A baby may suffocate from lying face-down on a soft pillow.

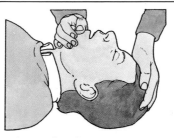

Immediately remove any obstructions to breathing, and check that the airway is open. Begin mouth-to- mouth resuscitation if necessary.

When breathing restarts, turn into the recovery position. Get medical help immediately.

Fire

A victim asphyxiated in a fire must be dragged clear to a safe place. Burning or smoldering clothing must be extinguished. Make sure you are not in danger.

If the victim is unconscious, turn them to the recovery position. If breathing or heartbeat have stopped, begin resuscitation. Send for medical help and treat any burns (see pages 36–7).

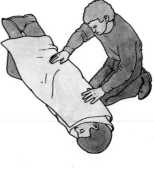

Drowning

Clear any obstructions from the victim's mouth and begin mouth-to-mouth resuscitation immediately.

If the water is shallow enough to stand, don't waste time by waiting to remove the victim from the water—start resuscitation immediately. In deeper water, give an occasional breath of air while towing the victim ashore. Check breathing and heartbeat.

If breathing returns, but the victim remains unconscious, turn into the recovery position. Keep warm and get medical help.

Gas-filled room

Make sure you are not in danger. Use a life line, so a helper can pull you clear if

you are overcome. Holding your breath, open window or break glass. Turn off gas appliance if possible.

Drag victim clear, and begin mouth-to-mouth resuscitation if breathing has stopped. Get medical help.

And this means that you, too, will be exposed to the situation which caused the original accident. So you must be aware that both your own life and that of the victim are at stake.

First aid will consist of clearing the airway, checking for breathing and heartbeat, and treating if necessary. The unconscious victim is placed always in the recovery position once breathing has been re-established.

Choking

Choking is the result of food or some other object lodging in the throat and blocking the airway. If the obstruction cannot be "coughed up," give four hard slaps on the back, between the shoulders. If this does not work, lean the victim well forward and repeat the four slaps.

Choking happens when the airway becomes blocked by a solid object, and the dangers are the same as drowning or suffocation. Choking is usually caused by a lump of food which has "gone down the wrong way" and been inhaled. It can also be caused by dentures slipping down the back of the throat or, in young children, by a small toy lodged in the throat.

You can recognize the signs of someone choking—they usually reach for their throat and are unable to speak. If the obstruction is not removed quickly, they become blue in the face, and the blood vessels in the neck and face bulge.

The obstruction is nearly always dislodged by coughing, but if not, a few hard slaps on the back can often jolt it out.

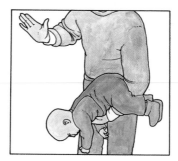

Babies and small children can be laid along the forearm or across the thigh, head down, and slapped lightly on the back four times.

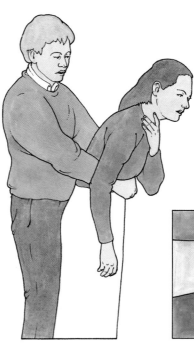

You must act *quickly*. First look to see whether anything is in the victim's mouth. If so, quickly hook it out with your fingers. Next get the victim to lean forward as far as possible (or upside down in the case of a baby) and give four smart slaps between the shoulder blades.

If breathing does not restart promptly, you may need to use a technique called the abdominal thrust, or **Heimlich maneuver**. This involves giving four sharp thrusts to the abdomen, forcing air out of the lungs and carrying the obstruction with it. If you cannot remove the obstruction, begin mouth-to-mouth resuscitation. This will usually force air past the obstruction until help can be obtained.

If the obstruction to breathing cannot be removed by simpler means, the abdominal thrust, or Heimlich maneuver, can be used. Stand behind the victim, wrap the arms around the abdomen, and grasp one clenched fist with the other hand. Pull inward and upward sharply, so the abdomen is compressed by the fists, usually shooting the obstruction free. In a child, the same effect is obtained using only one clenched hand, and proportionately less force.

Bleeding

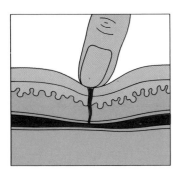

For almost all types of bleeding, applying pressure to the wound helps the blood to clot by slowing the rate of bleeding. Pressure on the skin over the wound flattens the blood vessels and limits the amount of blood flow, so clotting can take place.

Blood in the **arteries** is under the greatest pressure, so arterial bleeding is more serious than that from **veins** because blood is lost more quickly.

Blood is pumped around the body under pressure, so any break in the blood vessels allows blood to escape.

The body has its own system for dealing with most bleeding. When blood from a wound is exposed to the air, clotting begins. This normally slows the bleeding, producing a scab which seals the wound while healing takes place.

In a serious wound, blood may not clot fast enough to prevent the loss of a lot of blood. The victim may also be suffering from shock (see page 24), which can be dangerous unless treated.

For any bleeding wound, direct pressure reduces blood loss. By pressing firmly on the wound, the blood vessels beneath the skin are flattened, and blood flow is reduced. This gives time for blood clots to start forming, sealing off the damaged blood vessels.

You will need to apply pressure for from five to ten minutes, or longer if a very serious wound is involved. Don't be in too much of a hurry to remove pressure. When you do, watch to see whether bleeding starts again. If the injured part can be lifted and supported, this will help to reduce the blood flow.

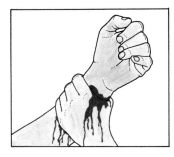

1 Apply direct pressure to the wound with the fingers. Maintain this pressure until bleeding stops, which may be 15 minutes or more.

2 Raise the injured part above the level of the heart and hold it in this position.

3 Put a **sterile** dressing over the wound and secure it with bandages or plasters.

4 If the bleeding starts again, do not remove the dressing; place another one over the top and re-bandage.

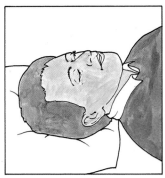

5 Watch for signs of shock, and get medical treatment.

There may be a foreign object in the wound, such as a piece of glass. If so, do not try to remove it, as it may be plugging the wound and you could make the bleeding worse. Instead, apply pressure around the wound, and get proper medical care for the victim.

Shock

Shock is a serious condition in which the blood supply to various organs and tissues fails, or becomes insufficient, causing a state of general collapse. It can be caused by loss of blood, or by failure of the heart to pump blood efficiently, as can happen after a **heart attack**.

A person in shock feels weak and has "cold sweats," with pale, clammy skin. Breathing and pulse become rapid but shallow, and the victim often yawns and sighs. If not treated promptly, the condition can deteriorate into unconsciousness. The victim must be treated to stop any bleeding, and reassured to prevent panic. He or she must be kept comfortably warm (but **not** with the use of hot-water bottles), and the feet should be raised slightly. Loosen tight clothing.

When signs of shock are seen:
1 Stop any bleeding.
2 Make victim comfortable and turn head to one side.
3 Raise and support the feet, and loosen tight clothing.
4 Maintain normal body temperature.
5 Send for medical assistance.

Cover and keep the victim warm and comfortable. Do not give anything to drink, and do not warm him with a hot-water bottle.

Do not give the victim anything to eat or drink.

If the victim loses consciousness, place in the recovery position and keep checking breathing and pulse every few minutes.

25

Electric shock

Electrical injuries are particularly dangerous. Electricity can cause severe burns to those parts of the skin where it enters and leaves the body. The current may also stop the heartbeat.

A person who has received an electric shock may have only a small burn visible on the skin but a larger area of damage beneath it. They may be unconscious, and their breathing and heartbeat can be affected. Physical shock is also common and will need treatment.

If you have to deal with someone who has received an electric shock, your first job is to make sure that it is safe to touch the victim. If there is still contact with the source of the shock, you could be electrocuted yourself. Pull out the plug if this is possible. Otherwise you must push the victim away from the source of current, **making sure you are well insulated**. This means standing on a dry surface and pushing the victim clear with a piece of wood. You must not attempt first aid until you are certain that electrical contact has been broken.

Now you can safely carry out the usual resuscitation procedures, and turn the victim into the recovery position.

1 Begin resuscitation immediately if victim is not breathing.
2 Place in recovery position if victim is breathing but unconscious.
3 Treat burns.
4 Look for shock and treat if necessary.
5 Get medical assistance.

In cases of electric shock, your first priority is to break the circuit to protect the victim and yourself. To do this you must stand on an insulated surface, and push the victim away from the source of the electricity, using a stick which will not conduct electricity. Do *not* touch the victim until you are certain that there is no risk.

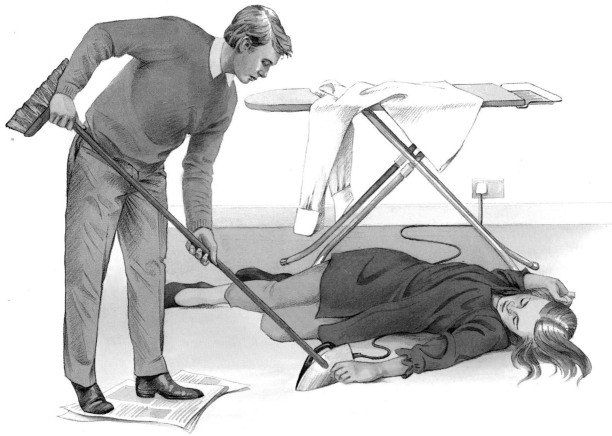

Common medical emergencies

There are several medical conditions which can cause a person to collapse or require some first-aid help. These can be frightening to onlookers, but are seldom dangerous to the victim. However, it is sensible to know what has caused the problem and what, if anything, needs to be done. Frequently the traditional ways of treating these conditions have been proved wrong, and even dangerous.

Asthma attack
Most people with asthma are receiving treatment and know how to cope with an attack. They should be reassured and sat down, leaning forward slightly, resting while the attack subsides. If the victim has medication, this should be taken at once.

Hysteria
Hysteria is a panicky over-reaction to a situation, when a person may become uncontrollably excited, or may be in a trance-like state. Try to get a hysterical person to sit down quietly, away from onlookers (which only makes the victim more excited). When they are calmer, reassure them and advise them to see the doctor.

Migraine
This is a very severe form of throbbing headache which can cause disturbance of vision and nausea. A cold compress against the forehead may help, together with pain-killing tablets. A rest in a darkened room is also helpful.

Fainting

Fainting is a brief loss of consciousness, which can be caused by shock or fear, pain, or sometimes by standing still for a long time. Recovery is quick if the victim can lie down, with the feet raised a little. Do not give anything to drink. Fainting can often be avoided by sitting down, leaning forward with the head between the knees. Tight clothing should be loosened.

Epileptic seizure

A person who is having a seizure will usually collapse unconscious, stiffen, and shake or tremble violently. There is very little to be done, and the victim will normally recover without assistance. If possible clear a space around the victim so that they do not incur injury, but do not try to restrain their movements or open the mouth. Loosen their clothing. Turn the victim into the recovery position when the seizure is over.

Diabetic coma

A person with diabetes occasionally collapses when the sugar level in their blood gets too low. When this happens, if they are still conscious, they must be given sugary drinks or candy to restore the proper sugar levels, and will recover quickly. If they are unconscious, they should be turned into the recovery position and medical help called *immediately*.

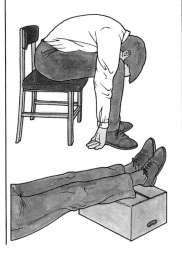

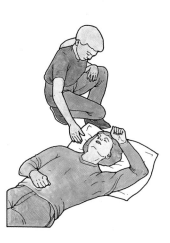

Epilepsy, for example, is a condition which sometimes causes a seizure, in which the victim falls to the ground and shakes violently. Many people try to restrain these movements, but this is quite unnecessary and may cause injury. Similarly, slapping people suffering from **hysteria** will not "bring them round," as many people believe. In all of the conditions described here, the wrong first-aid treatment is worse than no treatment at all.

Sprains and fractures

A cold compress applied to a sprain or to a bruise will help prevent painful swelling. A cold compress can be made by wrapping ice cubes in a cloth and pressing this against the injured part. In an emergency, a packet of frozen peas or similar freezer produce can be used!

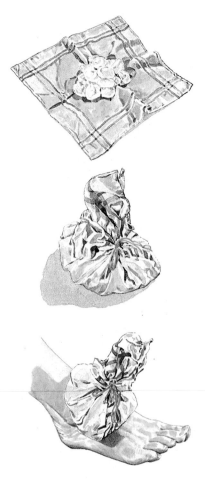

Joints are held together with tough fibers called ligaments, and if the joint is bent too far, or too violently, these may tear. This causes a very painful condition called a sprain, which can be mistaken for a broken bone if the tear is very bad. When this happens, fluid leaks into the damaged joint, making it swollen and very painful.

Raise the damaged part to reduce the blood flow, and apply a cold compress, which will prevent excessive swelling. This may be a bag containing ice, a towel soaked in cold water, or even a package of frozen peas from the freezer. The damaged joint then has to be immobilized, by wrapping it firmly in a bandage. Proper medical examination will be necessary to make sure that there are no broken bones.

If a bone is broken, pain and damage can be very severe. First-aid measures are all aimed at keeping the damaged parts immobile until help can be obtained. It is important not to move the victim, unless they are in obvious danger from traffic. Limbs can be immobilized by binding legs together, or by binding the arm against the side.

Any broken or severely sprained limb must be kept still. There are special first-aid techniques for this, but usually a splint can be improvised by simply tying the damaged limb firmly to a stick until medical help can be obtained. If no splint is available, a damaged leg can be tied to the other leg, or an arm tied against the side.

Moving a broken bone could cause great damage to the nerves and blood vessels alongside the break. You must treat any bleeding, and if the broken bone protrudes through the skin, it must be covered by a clean dressing. Shock is always a potential threat.

Cuts and bruises

Cuts
Minor cuts may not need any treatment, provided they are washed under running water to remove dirt. If the bleeding does not stop quickly, press a dressing over the cut until bleeding stops, then cover with an adhesive dressing.

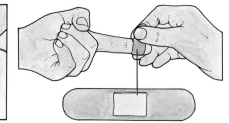

Bruises
A bruise is caused by bleeding under the skin, which produces swelling and discoloration. A bruise cannot be prevented, but applying a cold compress immediately after the injury will reduce the amount of bruising.

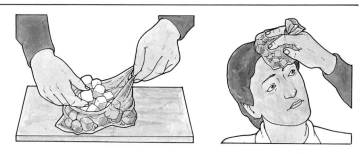

Abrasions
Abrasions must be washed carefully under running water. Remove any dirt, and swab gently with a gauze pad, brushing away from the center of the wound. Cover the abrasion with a sterile dressing and fasten with a bandage.

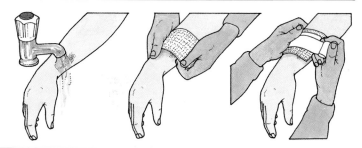

Nosebleed
Make the victim sit down, pinch the nostrils together, and lean forward. The bleeding normally stops within 10 to 20 minutes. Any blood trickling down the back of the throat should be spit out to avoid vomiting. Avoid blowing the nose for several hours.

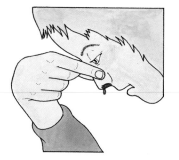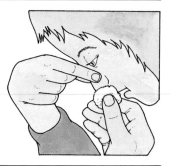

Sunburn

Move the victim out of the sun, and into some cool shade. Sponge the victim down with cold water, give plenty of cold water to drink, and apply after-sun cream to the burned areas. If the victim is badly blistered, get medical help.

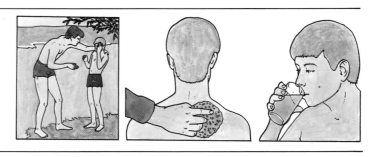

Splinters

Wash around the wound with soap and water. Sterilize a pair of tweezers by passing them through a flame, but do not wipe off the soot afterwards. Grip the splinter and pull out along the same path that it went in. If too deep to remove, don't try to dig it out; get medical attention.

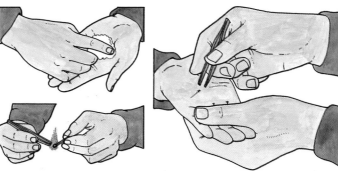

Fish-hook injuries

Cut the line, then turn the hook until the point comes out through the skin. Cut off the point and barb with wire cutters, then twist the hook gently out, along the path it entered. Get medical help.

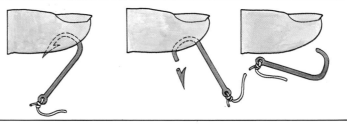

Blisters

Burn blisters need medical treatment, but you may be able to treat friction blisters. If these have burst, they can be cleaned and covered, like any minor wound.

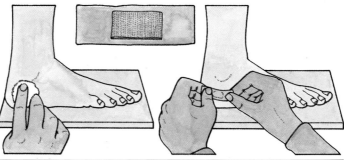

33

Bites and stings

Bee stings
If a bee or other insect stings, and leaves part of its sting embedded in the skin, this must be removed like a splinter. But it must not be gripped at its tip, as this would squeeze the poison sac and squirt more venom into the wound. Grip the stinger from the side and pull out carefully. Apply a cold compress to reduce swelling, and seek medical advice if the pain and swelling last for more than a couple of days.

Sting in the mouth
This can be dangerous if swelling develops. Tell the victim to suck ice cubes to minimize the swelling, or rinse the mouth with cold water. If breathing becomes obstructed, put the victim in the recovery position. Get medical help.

Sea-urchin spines
Sea-urchin spines can pierce the sole of the foot and break off in the skin. The spines can sometimes be withdrawn in the same direction as they entered, but if they break off beneath the skin, medical attention is needed to remove them.

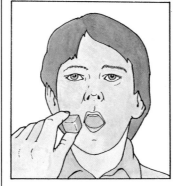

Jellyfish stings
Jellyfish stings are quite common when swimming in warm seas. Aspirin will relieve the pain, and **antihistamine** cream may help relieve itching.

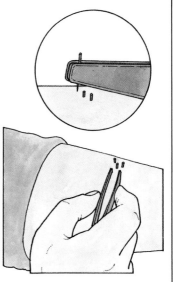

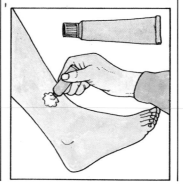

Snake bite

Fortunately snake bites are very rare. In susceptible people the effects of shock are more damaging than the venom. The victim should be reassured, and laid down. The bitten area must be immobilized and kept *below* the level of the heart. If victim loses consciousness, place in the recovery position. If breathing stops, give resuscitation. Wash the wound thoroughly, cover it with a dressing, and get the victim to a hospital as fast as possible.

Anaphylactic shock

Anaphylactic shock is a very severe and dangerous allergic reaction which very occasionally develops after repeated exposure to insect stings or to other bites. The victim collapses after a bite or sting, and must be treated promptly for shock, and taken to a hospital immediately. Ensure that breathing and heartbeat are maintained.

Dog bite

Bites from dogs or other animals need proper medical treatment, as they often become infected. Shallow bites should be washed with soapy water for at least 5 minutes, then covered with a dressing. For deeper bites, press to control bleeding, and cover with a dressing. For either shallow or deep bites, always get medical attention to prevent infection.

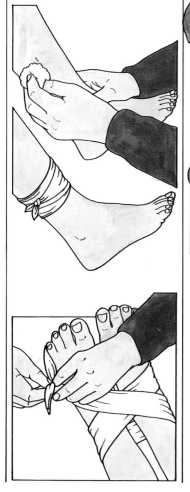

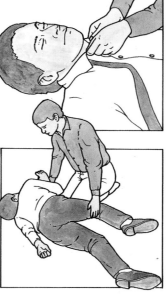

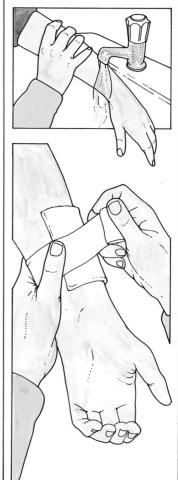

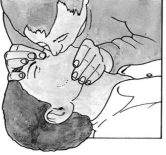

35

Burns and scalds

With minor burns, damage can be minimized by holding the injured part under cold water for 10 to 20 minutes. This also reduces pain and swelling. Chemical burns should be flushed with cold water. The injury must then be covered with a clean dressing and given proper medical treatment.

Burns can be caused in several ways. Flame or direct heat, corrosive chemicals like acids, electricity, excess sunbathing and friction can all cause burns of varying degrees. A shallow or superficial burn causes redness, while a more serious burn will cause blistering, when fluid leaks through the damaged skin. In the most serious burns, the skin is charred and blackened. Apart from a small superficial burn, all burns need proper medical treatment. Shock and infection are common in burns, especially when they cover a large area, and all burns are very painful.

For all burns, the principles of first aid are similar, which are to cool the area as fast as possible, and to prevent the entry of germs to the wound.

First, further burn damage must be prevented by extinguishing burning clothes or removing the victim from the source of the burn. Cool a mild burn by holding it under cold water for 10 to 20 minutes. The coolness will also reduce pain. Do not attempt to remove burned clothing or material sticking to the wound, but if the burn is caused by a scald or by corrosive chemicals, affected

If clothes are on fire, the victim should be made to lie down so that flames cannot lick around the face and wrapped in a coat or blanket to extinguish the flames. Do not try to remove any burned material from the wound.

clothing should be carefully removed, making sure you do not burn yourself.

The burn must be covered with a clean (preferably sterile) dressing, held in place with a light bandage. Burned hands or feet can be covered with clean dressings, taped into place. Watch for signs of shock, and get the victim to a doctor as fast as possible.

It is important to protect a burned area from further injury or infection by covering it with a sterile dressing. If this is not available, use a clean cloth. Always seek proper medical attention for all but the most superficial burns.

Extremes of temperature

In cases of frostbite it is essential to warm the frozen parts as quickly as possible. This is best done by using your own body heat, warming the victim against your own skin.

Exposure to extremes of temperature can cause several types of medical problems needing first aid.

Heat exhaustion is a condition caused by loss of body fluids and salt, usually through excessive perspiration in a hot climate. Victims have many of the symptoms of shock, including clammy, pale skin. They should be moved to a cool place and given sips of cool water to drink, with a half teaspoonful of salt added to each quart of liquid to help replace body salt. Medical aid must be obtained.

Heatstroke is a dangerous condition in which the body is unable to control its temperature, which may rise very suddenly. It can follow exposure to the sun, or some infections. The victim is very hot and may lose consciousness, though with a strong pulse. The temperature must be reduced immediately by placing the victim in a cool place, and sponging with cold or tepid water. The victim must be fanned continuously until the temperature is near normal. Place in the recovery position and obtain medical assistance as soon as possible.

Violent exertion in hot weather can cause heat exhaustion. This can be serious and it is important to get out of the sun and cool the body as rapidly as possible. Drink plenty of cold water or soft drinks.

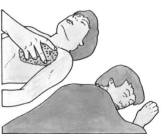

The opposite extreme is injury caused by cold. **Frostbite** is caused by the narrowing of blood vessels supplying the skin. Numbness occurs and the skin turns white or grayish-yellow. In **hypothermia**, the body temperature drops, and the victim becomes very cold and eventually loses consciousness. In both cases there is an urgent need to restore the proper temperature.

Young children sometimes suffer from overheating, and have a convulsion. This can occur after an infection, or even through over-excitement. The clothes must be loosened, and the child cooled by sponging down with tepid water. Don't let the child become too cold. Put him or her in the recovery position and get medical help.

Eye damage

Eye injury is always serious, as the eyes are delicate and can be permanently damaged if not properly treated after injury.

The most common eye injury does not actually affect the eye itself. This is a "black eye." Bruising around the socket causes the skin surrounding the eye to become discolored.

A black eye is painful and unsightly. There is little to be done to clear it up, but the damage can be reduced if a cold compress is applied immediately after the injury. A medical check-up is essential as there could be damage to the bones of the skull.

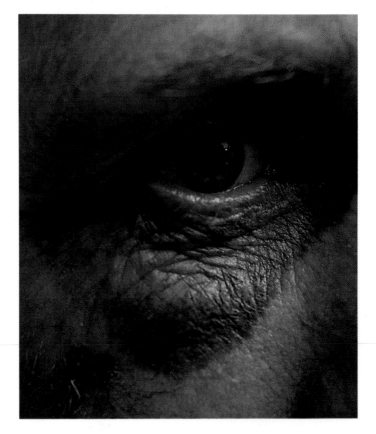

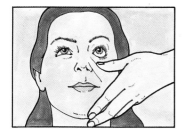

1 To remove a foreign object from the eye, get the victim to sit down, and tilt the head back. Wash your hands before starting first aid. Ask the victim to look up, then gently pull the lower eyelid down.

2 You may now be able to see the object on the white of the eye. Try to lift it off with the corner of a clean handkerchief.

3 If the object is under the upper eyelid, get the victim to look down. Pull the upper eyelid gently out and down over the lower lid. If this does not remove the object, get the victim to blink under water. Failing this, get medical help.

If foreign objects such as grit or an eyelash get into the eye, this can be painful. Never rub the eye, as this can scratch its surface. Foreign objects are frequently washed out by tears before treatment can be given. The painful itching that remains results from small scratches on the sensitive eye surface. Detailed instructions for the removal of foreign objects are given above.

If actual eye injury has occurred, or if the object is stuck to the eye or is on the colored center of the eye, this is a medical emergency, and you must not attempt to treat it.

The eye must be covered with a clean dressing, and medical attention obtained immediately. Chemical burns to the eye must be washed with cold water for 15 minutes. The eye should then be covered with a dressing, and given proper medical treatment.

First aid and the elderly

Elderly people can suffer the same types of accident as anyone else, but because of their age, some types of accident are more likely to affect them than a younger person.

Many elderly people are unsteady on their feet. If they trip, they may not be able to change their position quickly enough to avoid a fall. Their bones are more brittle than those of a young person, and can break very easily. For this reason it is important that staircases have proper handrails, and that loose pieces of carpet are secured.

Cold or hypothermia is a great hazard for the elderly in winter. Their bodies do not control temperature very well, and body temperature can drop to dangerous levels if rooms are not well heated. If you know older people living alone and you think that they may not be keeping warm during cold weather, call to check on them, and ask your family if any help can be given.

Old people are proud and often do not like to ask for help. Never be afraid to offer your assistance, and if you find an old person in obvious distress call for help immediately.

For an old person, a fall can be very serious. Bones become brittle in the elderly and break easily. Many old people are unsteady on their feet, and if they trip, are no longer agile enough to stop a fall. Medical help must always be sought, even if there are no obvious serious injuries.

43

Accidental poisoning

The home is where most accidents occur. Falls, burns, electric shock and cuts can happen in the home or anywhere else, but medical emergencies like poisoning are much more likely to take place in the home.

A kitchen cupboard is likely to contain a large range of poisonous or unpleasant substances, such as bleach, detergents and cleaning chemicals.

Most people are aware that certain mushrooms can be very poisonous, but young children may be tempted by them. Mushroom poisoning requires immediate hospital treatment.

Children are sometimes tempted by the poisonous seeds of the Laburnum tree, mistaking them for peas. Hospital treatment is needed for Laburnum poisoning.

The sap of the popular houseplant Dieffenbachia causes burning and temporary paralysis of the mouth and tongue, giving the plant its common name of Dumb Cane. It must be kept away from babies and pets.

Some of these substances are corrosive, burning the skin and eyes or, if they are eaten or drunk, causing internal burns. All chemicals must be kept away from children.

If accidental poisoning has occurred, try to find out what has been taken. Don't try to make victims vomit; instead give them milk or water to drink. If they are unconscious, turn the victim to the recovery position, but give mouth-to-mouth resuscitation if breathing stops. If there is any sign of blistering around the mouth of the victim; wash the area very thoroughly to avoid contaminating yourself during resuscitation. Get medical assistance immediately.

Brightly colored medical drugs are sometimes mistaken for candy, causing many cases of poisoning each year in young children. Drugs must always be kept in a safe place out of reach of children—preferably in a locked cupboard, stored in "childproof" bottles.

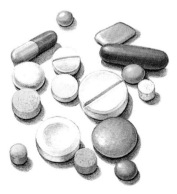

Glossary

A, B, C: The three important first-aid principles to follow when dealing with an unconscious victim. **A:** keep the airway clear. **B:** maintain breathing. **C:** maintain circulation by restarting the heart if necessary and by treating shock and bleeding.

Airway: the passage leading from the mouth, nose and throat to the windpipe through which air travels to the lungs. This passageway must be clear and open for breathing to take place.

Anaphylactic shock: a severe allergic reaction which sometimes affects people who have been sensitized to an insect sting by having been repeatedly stung on previous occasions.

Antihistamine: a substance which reverses the effects of an allergic reaction. Antihistamine creams can be used to treat several types of skin inflammation.

Artery: thick-walled blood vessel which carries blood away from the heart. Because blood carried by an artery is under pressure, bleeding from a cut artery is serious. Arterial blood is bright red, due to the oxygen it carries.

Asphyxiation: a condition in which there is not enough oxygen in the blood. It can be caused by a blocked airway or by a shortage of oxygen in the air, if a room is filled with smoke or gas.

Asthma: narrowing of the air passages in the lungs, usually caused by an allergic reaction. This makes it difficult to breathe during an asthmatic attack.

Diabetes: disease caused by a failure of the body to control the amount of sugar in the blood. A person with diabetes can collapse if the sugar level in the blood becomes too low.

Epilepsy: disease in which the brain produces sudden bursts of nerve impulses, which can cause the muscles to contract, producing a seizure or convulsion. A convulsion usually ceases without treatment.

External heart compression: technique for applying pressure to restart the heart when it has stopped beating. It must be used correctly to avoid causing further damage and must never be used if the heart is beating.

Frostbite: condition in which the tissues, usually of fingers and toes, become so cold that blood flow ceases, and they can then become frozen.

Heart attack: damage to the heart caused by blockage of the arteries supplying blood to the heart muscle.

Heat exhaustion: condition caused by loss of body fluids and salt due to sweating, usually in very hot weather and during vigorous exercise.

Heatstroke: a serious condition in which the body is unable to control a rapid rise in temperature in very hot weather or after an infection. The victim becomes very hot and may lose consciousness.

Heimlich maneuver: special technique to deal with someone who is choking. By pressing sharply on the abdomen, air is forced out of the lungs, carrying the obstruction with it and clearing the airway.

Hypothermia: a drop in body temperature to a dangerously low level, caused by exposure to cold. It is a risk in elderly people who do not keep their homes sufficiently warm and is also a hazard to people exposed to prolonged cold outdoors.

Hysteria: condition of overexcitement, fear, or panic, which causes a person to lose control of their emotions.

Migraine: very painful headache thought to be caused by temporary interference to the blood flow to the brain. It can cause sickness, and may temporarily interfere with vision.

Mouth-to-mouth resuscitation: is a technique for blowing air from the lungs into the lungs of a person who has stopped breathing.

Pulse: each time the heart beats it sends a strong spurt of blood along the arteries. This pulse can be felt wherever arteries lie close beneath the skin, for example in the neck and at the wrist.

Recovery position: position into which an unconscious victim is turned so they can continue to breathe without risk of the tongue or vomit blocking the airway.

Shock: condition in which the circulation begins to fail, first causing unconsciousness, but sometimes causing death if not treated properly.

Sterile: a sterile dressing is one which has been treated to destroy any bacteria or other organisms which could cause disease if they entered a wound.

Sternum: the breastbone, connecting the ribs at the front of the chest.

Suffocation: see Asphyxiation.

Sunburn: burning caused by the effects of ultraviolet radiation in sunlight. It causes redness, blistering, and can sometimes result in severe skin burns.

Vein: a thin-walled blood vessel returning blood to the heart. Blood from a damaged vein is much darker than the bright red blood from an artery.

Index